READING
AND
MAKING
NOTES

POCKET STUDY SKILLS

Series Editor: **Kate Williams**, *Oxford Brookes University, UK*

Illustrations by Sallie Godwin

For the time-pushed student, the *Pocket Study Skills* pack a lot of advice into a little book. Each guide focuses on a single crucial aspect of study giving you step-by-step guidance, handy tips and clear advice on how to approach the important areas which will continually be at the core of your studies.

Published

14 Days to Exam Success

Blogs, Wikis, Podcasts and More

Brilliant Writing Tips for Students

Getting Critical

Planning Your Essay

Planning Your PhD

Reading and Making Notes

Referencing and Understanding Plagiarism

Science Study Skills

Success in Groupwork

Further titles are planned

Pocket Study Skills

Series Standing Order
ISBN 978-0230-21605-1
(outside North America only)

You can receive future titles in this series as they are published by placing a standing order. Please contact your bookseller or, in case of difficulty, write to us at the address below with your name and address, the title of the series and the ISBN quoted above.

Customer Services Department, Macmillan Distribution Ltd Houndmills, Basingstoke, Hampshire RG21 6XS England

POCKET STUDY SKILLS

Jeanne Godfrey

READING AND MAKING NOTES

palgrave
macmillan

First published 2010 by
PALGRAVE MACMILLAN

Palgrave Macmillan in the UK is an imprint of Macmillan Publishers Limited, registered in England, company number 785998, of Houndmills, Basingstoke, Hampshire RG21 6XS.

Palgrave Macmillan in the US is a division of St Martin's Press LLC, 175 Fifth Avenue, New York, NY 10010.

Palgrave Macmillan is the global academic imprint of the above companies and has companies and representatives throughout the world.

Palgrave® and Macmillan® are registered trademarks in the United States, the United Kingdom, Europe and other countries

ISBN-13: 978-0-230-24758-1

This book is printed on paper suitable for recycling and made from fully managed and sustained forest sources. Logging, pulping and manufacturing processes are expected to conform to the environmental regulations of the country of origin.

A catalogue record for this book is available from the British Library.

A catalog record for this book is available from the Library of Congress.

10 9 8 7 6 5 4 3 2 1
19 18 17 16 15 14 13 12 11 10

Printed in China

Contents

Acknowledgements

My thanks go to all my students, past and present and future, for helping me along the road of insight into reading and making notes, and for providing me with the reason for writing this guide.

I am grateful to Kate Williams for asking me to write this book and for her fantastic support. I would also like to thank Sallie Godwin for her excellent and humorous sketches, which really bring the text to life.

Thanks also to the Palgrave Macmillan team for their friendly and professional work with me on this book, particularly Suzannah Burywood and Caroline Richards.

The extract from the report on Guideline Daily Amounts by Lobstein, Landon and Lincoln is reproduced with the kind permission of the National Heart Forum, and the article extract by A. Oswald is reproduced with kind permission from Wiley-Blackwell Publishing.

Introduction

Reading and making notes form the foundations of a great deal of university study, and this pocket guide will take you quickly and clearly through the key points of these two key activities. Confidence comes from knowing *what* to do and *how* to do it, but when you start out at university you may not know exactly what is expected of you. You may, for example, hold some of these common beliefs about university study.

10 myths about reading and making notes at university

#1 You need to read most things on your reading list, starting at the top and working your way down.

#2 In your first year you will be reading and writing assignments rather than doing research.

#3 All books and articles are well written and truthful.

#4 You should read academic texts* carefully from start to finish.

* 'text' is a general term for any type of written document. Other words with similar meanings used in this guide are 'source' 'reading material' and 'the literature'.

#5 There is only one correct way to understand a text.

#6 You can't really disagree with an academic text because you are not an expert in that subject.

#7 If you don't understand something or feel confused, it is probably because you are being a bit thick.

#8 Intelligent people and good readers usually only need to read things once.

#9 You should look up all the words you don't understand as you go along.

#10 Good notes should have all the points from the text copied down.

This pocket guide will explode these myths one by one. It will tell you exactly what your university tutors *do* expect of you and what you need to do to meet these expectations. I want you to be able to hit the ground running from the very start of your studies, to get the best marks possible for your work, and to make the best possible use of your talents, your tutors and your time.

No matter what your starting point is, you could probably read and make notes more effectively by adjusting or adding to your current reading strategies. This guide gives you practical advice and uses real assignment titles, reading lists and text extracts. It also looks at real tutor feedback and university marking criteria.

Reading for study can actually be an enjoyable experience, and I hope that using this pocket guide will help you to feel more confident and relaxed about this aspect of your work.

PART 1

WHAT IS THE PURPOSE OF READING AT UNIVERSITY?

1 What your lecturers are looking for

Below is a table that summarises the main differences between reading at school or college and reading for university study.

School and college	University
The readings for assessments are usually set, managed and prioritised by the teacher.	*You* are expected to decide what to read and what *not* to read.
All students read the same texts.	Because of the choices you make, some or all of the sources you read will be different from those other students read for the same assignment.

School and college	University
Students learn mainly by absorbing the information in the texts and repeating it in different forms.	You are expected to think beyond the information in the texts and to make up your own mind about *whether* the information is important, *why* it is important and *how* it connects with other information and ideas.

Let's look at the 'university' column in a bit more detail. Producing excellent assignments involves a process that has many different stages to it, most of which centre around your reading. It's a bit like building a house. You need to know what the design brief is (your assignment) and to build your house brick by brick, using good quality materials (your sources) and good workmanship.

The brick wall diagram opposite gives an illustration of how you need to build upwards from the solid foundation of understanding your assignment title.

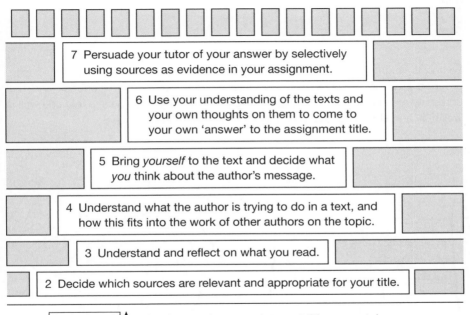

7 Persuade your tutor of your answer by selectively using sources as evidence in your assignment.

6 Use your understanding of the texts and your own thoughts on them to come to your own 'answer' to the assignment title.

5 Bring *yourself* to the text and decide what *you* think about the author's message.

4 Understand what the author is trying to do in a text, and how this fits into the work of other authors on the topic.

3 Understand and reflect on what you read.

2 Decide which sources are relevant and appropriate for your title.

Start here! ↑ 1 Understand your assignment title accurately.

Lecturers might use more formal language to describe these bricks. Opposite, grouped into the seven stages, are extracts from real lecturer feedback and real university marking criteria for excellent and for poor work. You can see that one wall is well built and strong but that the other is misshapen and crumbling!

	Good work	Poor work
7	'Evaluates evidence and synthesises materials clearly to develop persuasive arguments.' 'Evidence used appropriately to support their conclusion.'	'Baseless assertions.' 'Essay is over-reliant on too few sources.' 'Poorly used material.'
6	'... clear insight and independent thought.' 'An accurate and critically reflective treatment of all the main issues.'	'Uses mainly description rather than coming to a critical conclusion.'
5	'... willingness to engage critically with the literature and ability to go beyond it ...' '... mindful of other interpretations ...'	'... does not go beyond the assertion of points derived from the literature.'
4	'... clear understanding of the nature of the material.' '... ability to analyse materials and their implications.'	'... lack of awareness of the context of the material.'
3	'Sources used accurately and concisely but do not dominate...' '... good command of the literature ...'	'inaccurate reading and limited understanding ...'
2	'... evidence of ability to select appropriately ...' '... detailed *and* broad knowledge base.'	'Needs to refer to the relevant literature.' 'Some sources used are not academically rigorous.'
1	'Has interpreted the question fully and accurately.'	'... has not clearly understood the assignment task.'

Of course, you can't build a house with bricks alone – you need to use mortar to cement one brick to the next. The mortar of an assignment is thinking and writing (including scribbles, notes, pictures, diagrams, summaries, reflections and questions). The better the quality of your thinking and writing, the stronger your final assignment.

Before we go on to talk about how to meet your tutor's expectations, it's important to bear two things in mind. First of all, you will not be expected to do everything perfectly from the start. Your tutors will expect you to develop these abilities gradually during your first year and beyond, and will mark your work accordingly. The second thing to remember is that:

> 'The whole [university] system is set up to help you succeed – all you need to do is co-operate.' (Dixon 2004 p3)

You will have lots of help – your lecturers, other students, course handouts and reading lists, advice help sheets, personal tutors and your university library. Make the most of them!

Dixon TM (2004). *How to get a first: The essential guide to academic success.* Oxford: Routledge.

3   Active reading

One of the most important tools you will need to 'build' your assignment is an active approach to reading. Reading for study should not be a passive activity that you do only with your eyes – it requires active effort that engages your brain.

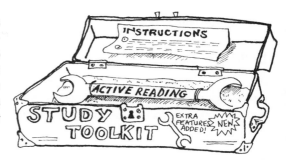

Have a clear purpose

Take responsibility for your own learning from the very start. Always ask yourself, 'Why am I going to look for/read/make notes on this?' You should know why you are reading a particular chapter or article and what you hope to get from it. At the start of your course your precise aims may be a little vague, but with practice you will be able to decide on a specific purpose for each text you read.

Make predictions

Before you start to read something in detail, make some predictions about what you expect to find. Predictions and expectations (even if they turn out to be wrong) will help engage your brain.

Build a scaffold

Always try to link what you read to what you already know about the subject, how it relates to other topics and how it relates to your own life experience. This is important, as you need to build a scaffold in your mind onto which you can attach new knowledge.

Challenge the author

Someone wrote each text you read. Think about who they are and why they might have written it. Have a conversation in your mind with the author before, during and after reading.

Engage and enjoy

Doing the three things above will get you involved in what you are reading. Engage and interact with the text – there should be a continuous two-way process of reading and thinking, and of putting together old and new information to reach your own unique understanding. React to what you read – you will enjoy it much more!

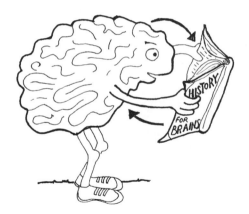

Don't be too hard on yourself if you find reading actively difficult at first. Don't forget that the experts in the field (including your lecturers) will have read and written about the same subjects for years and so will have developed large scaffolds which allow their brains to easily fit new information into what they already know.

Have the confidence to know that you too will gradually develop scaffolds and build up knowledge. Texts that at first seem alien will become easier as you go forward, but only if you build up your 'reading muscles' by – you guessed it – reading!

Summary

- The point of reading at university is to allow you to come to your own independent understanding of your subject.

- An excellent assignment is one that has been built properly, brick by brick.

- An excellent assignment will have a conclusion that is persuasive because it is based upon a strong argument that uses relevant and well-understood evidence.

- Having a clear purpose and goals for your reading will increase your motivation, which will in turn increase your level of understanding and thus your enjoyment.

- Build up your active reading muscles by practising active reading.

DECIDING WHAT AND WHAT *NOT* TO READ

Understand your assignment title

Understanding your assignment title is fundamental. Don't make the mistake of reading the title quickly, assuming you know what it means and then plunging into unfocused reading. Not understanding the title properly is a common cause of low assignment marks.

☑ 'has interpreted the question fully and accurately'

☒ 'has not clearly understood the assignment task'

For your assignment title, make sure you have clearly identified and understood:

> **C**: the **concept** words or phrases – words related to the content of the topic.
>
> **F**: the **function** words – does the title ask you to describe, analyse, argue, or some of these things together?
>
> **S**: the **scope** of the title – what you are asked to cover and not to cover. If the scope is not explicit in the title, you will need to decide on the scope yourself.

Use these three aspects to break down and to carefully analyse your title. Discuss it with fellow students and get advice from your tutor if you are still not sure what it means.

Let's have a look at two real assignment titles and see how the student has used these three aspects to understand them.

For more help with assignment titles, see *Planning your essay* and *Getting critical* in the Pocket Study Skills series.

Assignment title 1

Course   BSc Health and Human Sciences
First-year module 'Nutrition and Lifestyle'

Case study title

(C) illness caused by lifestyle - e.g. CHD, diabetes 2. I will choose coronary heart disease (CHD).

Your client has one of the *(C)* major lifestyle-related diseases.

(F) *(Outline)* the *(aetiology)* of the disease and *(give a critical account)* *(F)*

(F) brief summary only

of the *(measures)* that *(are being)* taken in *(the UK)* to prevent it.

Don't just describe! - how effective are they? Problems?

(C) causes

(C) <u>actions</u> e.g.
· policies
· legislation
· advice
· NHS/Schools...

(S) <u>now</u> (not past!)

(C) <u>not</u> worldwide U.S.A

Assignment title 2

Course   MSc in Economic Psychology
Seminar on 'Happiness and the Economy'

Essay title

(C) clear/statistical link

(C) i.e. a nation's economic state

To what extent is there (a correlation) between (an economy) of a society) and the (levels of happiness) experienced by that society?

(F)
- if there is a correlation, how strong is it?
- are there any exceptions to such a link?
- what are the problems/issues with trying to find a correlation?

(S) which society/ies? I will choose Western/developed societies.

(C) how happy people are

A clearer idea of what you need

Once you have analysed your assignment title you should be much clearer on exactly what you need to read about and what questions you want answered. You should also have a better idea about what *types* of sources you will need, such as:

▶ introductory textbooks

▶ key established works on the topic

▶ original data from experiments

▶ recent academic journal articles on new developments or ideas

▶ non-expert and/or public views from websites or newspapers.

At the start of your course you will probably be given a reading list and directed towards some specific background reading. Before long, however, you will be expected to use your reading list to make your own selection of sources for assignments.

> **Myth #1** You need to read most things on your reading list, starting at the top and working your way down.

Now that you have analysed your assignment title, you can approach your reading list in a purposeful way and decide what *you* want to read rather than letting your reading list control you. Your tutors do not want you to read everything on the reading list – they want to see that you can *discriminate* between sources (i.e. make good judgements) and to see an '... ability to select appropriately ...'.

Myth #2 In your first year you will be reading and writing assignments rather than doing research.

In fact, selecting and finding sources is a key part of academic research, and the uniqueness of your assignment starts when you make your own selection of sources.

Let's look at a section from the reading list for the 'Nutrition and Lifestyle' module. My comments on the list are given next to it.

> **Attention!** Notice that the lecturers do not always give the complete bibliographic details of the texts in their reading lists – you will be expected to complete these details yourself and you must always use the full bibliographic details of any source for your assignment bibliography and reference list. For more on how to reference, see *Referencing and understanding plagiarism* in the Pocket Study Skills series.

Reading list for 'Nutrition and Lifestyle'

The reading list below is for the module in general. You will need more specific readings for your chosen topic (please see departmental Key Texts collection and get guidance from your tutor if necessary).

Additionally, any textbook on biochemistry and nutrition. Also nutrition journals and a wide range of nutrition books in general.

Tutor's annotations – give big clues to relevant reading.

For your specific topic (CHD) select only relevant background reading from the list, look through the collection of Key Texts, and ask your tutor for advice on sources.

The latest editions of MAFF *Manual of Nutrition*, Food Standards Agency, London.

Topical Updates, Recommendations of:

FSA: www.foodstandards.gov.uk/

Committee on Medical Aspects of Food and Nutrition Policy (COMA).

Scientific Advisory Committee on Nutrition (SACN).

– look at these sites for latest government recommendations on dietary advice for preventing CHD.

Bessesen H and Kushner R (eds) *Evaluation and management of obesity.*

Fisher M (ed.) (2004) *Heart disease and diabetes.* London: Martin Dunitz.

Garrow JS (2000) (eds) *Human nutrition and dietetics.* Note – 10th edition.

← These three books all have editors (eds) and chapters written by different authors – common in the academic world. Select only relevant chapters. Key authors often write chapters in edited books that give a condensed version of their longer work – very useful!

Gibney MJ, Vorster H and Kok FJ (2002) *Introduction to human nutrition.* Blackwell Publishing.

← – introductory textbook – you will only need to quickly scan and then use parts of this to summarise nutritional-based causes of CHD.

McArdle W, Katch V and Katch F (2006) *Nutrition for sport and exercise.*

← – what you need to eat for *sport*. Not relevant to your assignment topic.

Veith VW (1998) *Diet and health: scientific perspectives.*

← Yes? Scientific perspectives may not be directly relevant but it's worth browsing the contents page.

Whitney et al. (1998) *Understanding normal and clinical nutrition.*

← 'Clinical nutrition' is a common term in this module so you should have checked out what it means by now. If you have, you will know that parts of this book will probably be relevant.

So, from this reading list there are three websites you would need to look at, two or three chapters from the edited books, parts of Gibney et al. and relevant sections of the last three books.

Look back at assignment title 1 – what reading gaps do you need to fill? You still need some sources on preventative measures other than nutrition (e.g. exercise) and some sources that discuss and evaluate these measures.

Let's now take a quick look at the reading list for the MSc Economic Psychology seminar.

Reading list for 'Happiness and the Economy'

Basic reading
EITHER Myers (1994) Who is happy – and why? (chap 11 of *Exploring Social Psychology*). … 2.930
OR Myers and Diener (1995) Who is happy? *Psychological Science* 6(1), 10–19.

– tutor has been very helpful – directing you to specific chapters, library catalogue numbers (2.930) and telling you which sources are held in the department. Also sometimes gives additional comments in brackets.

◄ – take tutor's advice – you only need one of these sources, not both.

Argyle M (1987) *The psychology of happiness*. Choose chapters. Departmental box.

Csikszentmihalyi M (1992) *Flow: the psychology of happiness*. Choose chapters ...

Lane RE (2002) *Political psychology*, chaps 22, 26 (and other chapters in Part VII if you've time).

Scitovsky (1992) *The joyless economy*, chap 4 (comfort versus pleasure).

> For all the other titles under basic reading, just scan for the chapters directly relevant to your title of economic performance and happiness.

Additional material

Oswald AJ (1997) Happiness and economic performance. *The Economic Journal* 107(445), 1815–31.

> – looks directly relevant.

Kaplan (1987) Lottery winners: the myth and the reality. *J Gamb Beh* 3, 168–78.

Brickman et al. (1978) Lottery winners and accident victims: Is happiness relative? *Journal of Personality and Social Psychology* 36, 917–27.

> These two titles are not relevant to your title. Individual wealth via winning the lottery does not directly relate to the general economy.

Veenhoven (1988) *National wealth and individual happiness*, pp867–82.

Scitovsky T (1992) *The joyless economy*, chaps 6, 8, 9, 10.

◄— Yes, these two titles look directly relevant – tutor is directing you to specific pages and chapters.

Frey and Stutzer (1999) Happiness, economy and institutions. This is coming out in the *Economic Journal*, October 2000, and can be downloaded from the Institute of Empirical Economics *Working Papers* page.

◄— Might be relevant, might not (depends how much emphasis is given to institutions). You may want to just look at the list of contents to reassure yourself that you don't need to read it.

So, from this reading list there will probably be about seven chapters and four articles that are useful. These would seem to give a good coverage for the assignment title; however, none of them are particularly recent and so you would also need to hunt around for more current sources.

Some other things to remember about reading lists

▶ You may get a thorough and helpful reading list or you may not – some lecturers expect you to do more detective work than others.

▶ Even with the 'required' or 'essential' reading section there may be titles that cover similar ground, so still be selective.

▶ If you want to ask your lecturer for guidance, don't expect them to tell you what to read. Do some thinking first and then ask your lecturer to comment on your choices.

▶ Reflect, even if briefly, on *all* the titles on your list, even the ones you reject – this will help you become familiar with authors and topics in the subject.

▶ Discuss sources with your fellow students – you're supposed to share references.

If the library doesn't have a copy of something you want ...

Don't panic. This is quite common, as few libraries can have enough copies for all students at all times. As we have seen, most reading lists will give you acceptable alternatives and you will find further similar titles through your own search. Reserve the title if it's out on loan and ask if there are any other university libraries you can use. You can also get advice from your tutor or other students and check online sites, bookshops and student notices for second-hand copies.

If you think you have a good range of suitable sources already, trying to find more just for the sake of it will be a waste of time. Stick to the rule of only searching for something if you have a clear purpose. Remember that your tutors want to see 'evidence of ability to select *appropriately*'. However, if done well and for the right reasons, going 'off-road' will get you good marks and will also help you build up a '... good command of the literature ...'.

We identified some source gaps (preventative measures other than nutrition, and evaluation of these measures) for assignment 1, so let's look at a selection of off-road sources found by searching under 'preventative measures for CHD in the UK'. Note that the student has recorded the full bibliographic details for each source.

Off-road sources found for assignment 1

Ananthaswamy A (2004) Eat less and keep disease at bay. *New Scientist* 182(2444), 24 April p11–12.

◀— No – already have enough sources on nutrition, and also *New Scientist* is a magazine and is not peer-reviewed.

Willett WC (2002). Balancing life-style and genomics research for disease prevention. *Science* 296(5568), 26 April p695–8.

◀— Yes? Has some of the right words in the title but look carefully – it's about balancing <u>research</u>, so no.

Morris JN et al. (1980) Vigorous exercise in leisure-time: protection against coronary heart disease. *Lancet* 8206 p1207–10.

◀— Yes/No? On exercise, good and *Lancet* is a peer-reviewed journal but a very medical/technical one – may not be appropriate.

Model Ali NS (2002) Prediction of coronary heart disease preventative behaviours in women: a test of the health belief. *Women and Health* 35(1), p83–96.

◀— Yes? – haven't yet considered differences between men and women – good but what type of journal is *Women and Health*?

Sources found on CHD and government/public policy

Brunner C, Cohen D and Toon L (2001) Cost effectiveness of cardiovascular disease prevention strategies: a perspective on EU food based dietary guidelines. *Public Health Nutrition* 4, p711–15.

◀— Yes? Effectiveness of preventative strategies – excellent – but is the EU directly relevant for the UK?

Calnan M (1991) *Preventing coronary heart disease: prospects, policies and politics.* London and New York: Routledge.

◄ Yes, spot on – will contain full discussions and evaluations of policies for preventing CHD.

Lobstein, Landon and Lincoln (2007) *Misconceptions and misinformation: The problems with Guideline Daily Amounts (GDAs).* National Heart Forum: www.heartforum.org.uk [Accessed 21/11/2010]

◄ Yes. Although related to nutrition, advice to public on food is a key preventative measure and we don't have anything on food labelling yet. But is NHF a reliable organisation and website?

NHS (2009) Avoiding coronary heart disease: http://www.nhs.uk [Accessed 22/11/2010]

◄ Yes. Reliable website for info. and advice that the NHS gives to the public.

So, this off-road search has found information on CHD public policy and other preventative measures, and on evaluations of these measures. The search has also brought up two new ideas – the role of genes and possible CHD differences between men and women – but you would need to check these sources more closely for relevance.

Myth #3 All books and articles are well written and truthful.

Notice that my comments on the off-road search include questioning whether the sources were reliable. At university it is *your* responsibility to check the reliability of any sources you use – that you can trust what they say. Make sure that:

- you know who wrote something and that they are an authority on their topic. Anonymous sources are much more likely to be of poor quality and/or contain incorrect information;

- your sources are up to date. You may want to read older sources but for most topics, current information will be more reliable;

- you are aware of possible bias. However, bear in mind what 'reliable' means for the type of information you need. For example, if your essay is about public opinion in the media, newspapers and television programmes will be reliable sources for this information;

- you get hold of the original (primary) source of information where possible, as something reported second or third hand will be less accurate and reliable. Find the original experiment, data or article rather than another report or article (a secondary source) that discusses the primary material. In reality, you will often use secondary sources, but you will usually also be expected to read the key primary texts on a topic.

What is an academic source?

❌ 'Some sources used are not academically rigorous.'

For most assignments you will need to use sources that are not only reliable but are also regarded as *academic*. This means sources written by experts (or authorities) that have gone through a peer-review process – the book or article is sent by the publisher to other experts for checking before publication. Peer-reviewed sources are reliable and are also described as academic, reputable or authoritative.

Books have usually had to go through a peer-review process, and a journal described as an 'academic', 'peer-reviewed' or 'scholarly' journal will be reliable and academic. It doesn't matter whether a journal is in print or online or both – what matters is whether it has been peer reviewed.

Source types that are *not* academically rigorous include:

▸ academic conference proceedings
▸ newspapers (even long articles in quality papers such as *The Times* or the *Guardian*)
▸ magazines (even quality magazines such as the *Economist*, *Newsweek* and *New Scientist*)
▸ trade publications and company websites
▸ publications and websites of charities, and of campaign or pressure groups
▸ student theses or essays
▸ Wikipedia.

Always check your online sources

▶ Some online databases contain only peer-reviewed academic journals but some of them (even one that describes itself as a 'research database') also contain newspapers, magazines and trade publications.

▶ You also need to check material you find through subject gateways such as Intute, DOAJ, HighWire, Zetoc Ingenta and Copac. Read the description of a database or gateway before you go into it – what does it say it contains? You may be able to google it and/or get a description of its publications on the 'home' or 'about us' page.

▶ Online search engines (Google, Alta Vista, Yahoo, Wolframalpha etc.) will obviously give you both reliable and unreliable material but you also need to check material you find through Google Scholar as it will include magazines and student theses.

▶ Wikipedia is a type of encyclopaedia and is therefore only a basic summary. It is a secondary or even tertiary source, is anonymous and is not peer reviewed – all things that make it unreliable and not academic. Wikipedia may be useful for some initial definitions and to give you links to other sources, but you should not use it as an actual source in your assignment.

- Always check that you know the author of any website you use. Who funds and supports the site? Is the purpose of the site made clear? Is any advertising clearly distinguished from the main text?

- Words such as *research journal* or *volume/issue number* are being increasingly used on unreliable and non-academic websites so don't rely on such descriptions.

- Words that should warn you that an online website or article is not academic are: *magazine, digest, personals, news, press release, correspondent, journalist, special report company, classified* and *advertisement*.

So, with the importance of reliability and academic rigour in mind, let's have a look at the results of an off-road search for assignment 2. After selecting from the reading list, we identified that we wanted to find some more up-to-date sources.

Off-road sources found for assignment 2

Graham C (2005) The economics of happiness. *World Economics* 6(3) p41–55. ← Yes? Spot on and relatively recent, but is *World Economics* peer reviewed?

Lyubomirsky S, King L and Diener E (2005) p803–55 The benefits of frequent positive affect: does happiness lead to success? *Psychological Bulletin* 131(6) p803–855. ← No. A peer-reviewed journal and more current, but the title shows that it's about how happy and successful *individuals* are rather than looking at whole *economies*.

Belle D, Doucet J, Harris J, Miller J and Tan E (2000) [comment/reply]: Who is rich? Who is happy? *American Psychologist* 55(10) p1160–61. ← No. Careful – looks good but is in fact only a comment/reply to another article – not reliable – would need to find the original article.

O'Brien, Catherine (2008) Sustainable happiness: how happiness studies can contribute to a more sustainable future. *Canadian Psychology/Psychologie canadienne* 49(4) p289–95. ← No. A peer-reviewed journal and sustainable happiness is an interesting angle – but the article is only about how more *studies* in this area could be useful.

So, this off-road search has found one useful current source and given us a couple of peer-reviewed journals for possible future use.

Make the most of your library

With so much stuff available online, some students don't go near their university library until the end of their second year or later. This is a real shame because your library can help you with some of the very problems that arise from information overload. Don't make the mistake of thinking that the internet is just like a big online library – it isn't!

Go to your library and get a demonstration of how the catalogue system works, which books and journals are available online, what the short loan section contains, how many items you can take out at once and what the late return penalties are.

Searching for sources using library resources and staff

Pros:

Material has already been pre-selected by lecturers and library staff for its importance, relevance, reliability and academic quality.

The intranet and library catalogue material (again, chosen by your tutors/library) is more likely to be reliable than material from the internet.

Library staff are there to help you with selecting and finding texts.

Has an online catalogue system that contains a list of all its resources. Will also give you free access to other academic online databases.

You can use the 'sort' facility of the library catalogue to put sources in order of publication.

Will have primary printed material and back copies of journals, newspapers and magazines that are not available online.

Will have specialist dictionaries, study guides and material written by your university not available online.

Provides a quiet and comfortable environment in which to study, away from distractions.

Free Wifi connection and use of DVDs.

Free use of magazines and newspapers, dictionaries, encyclopaedias and other print material.

Staff will be able to arrange for you to borrow from other libraries.

Cons:

The copies of a book or article may be out on loan (but you can reserve them!).

Searching for sources using only the internet

Pros:

A huge number of sources are available.

24-hour access (although your library may also be open nearly 24 hours).

Cons:

Search engines will often return a large number of returns and false matches and it can be hard to find the most relevant source.

Sometimes difficult to find out who wrote something and whether the source is reliable and peer reviewed.

A significant number of academic sources are not yet available online.

You often have to pay for downloads of complete books or articles.

9 Fine-tune your selection

This is an important stage that will save you a great deal of time. Collect your selection of sources and give each one a job interview. Does it have the correct expertise, qualifications and experience for what you want it to do?

Read the title, contents page, headings and sub-headings and go through the index to narrow down the sections that are specifically relevant to your needs. Quickly scan through the text, giving yourself a time limit. If you can't find the points you are looking for in the first 10–15 minutes then the text is probably not directly relevant.

You may feel that deciding not to read something is somehow being disrespectful to the author, but this is just how academic study works – you are simply identifying that what the author has written is not right for this particular job.

Reviews, abstracts and summaries

These are all useful in different ways to give you a general idea of a text, but remember that if you decide to use the source in your assignment you will need to read the text itself in order to be able to evaluate and critically discuss it.

Review	Written by someone else. If the review has been written by an expert, it may give you useful information about the context of the source and other published work in the field. However, reviews are of no use for detailed information and may often be a biased personal opinion.
Abstract	Always written by the author. Gives the outline topic but not always the conclusion. You will not be able to understand each step or be able to evaluate the evidence, argument or conclusion just by reading the abstract.
Summary	Could be written by the author or by someone else. Summarises the argument and the conclusion but not in enough detail for you to be able to evaluate the evidence or argument.
Introduction and conclusion	Written by the author. These give a good idea of the main points and argument but are not enough for you to evaluate the evidence or argument.

Sources checklist

So, before you start reading a source in detail you should be able to answer most of the following questions:

▶ What type of source is it?

▶ Who wrote it and when?

▶ Is it relevant, reliable and academic – and if not, is that OK?

▶ Is the main function of the text to describe, explain, hypothesise, argue, or some of these things together?

▶ Who is the text written for?

▶ Why are you going to read it – what exactly do you want to get out of it?

▶ Do you think it will support your conclusion or give an opposing viewpoint?

Keep a record of the titles of your sources *and* how and when you found them. The reasons for this are many: to build up your own research files, to be able to reference properly in your essay and avoid accidental plagiarism, to complete your bibliography, to show your tutor, to be able to easily find the source again if you need to and so that you can share a reference with a colleague.

This record is sometimes called a research log. You can use online software, keep a simple document file or even use index cards for your log. The important thing is that each log entry is complete. For books you must include the edition, the publisher and where it was published; the ISBN number is also useful. It should also be accurate: for example, do not change upper/lower case letters or punctuation in the title.

Here's an example of a research log entry:

Reference details: Oswald AJ (1997) Happiness and economic performance. *The Economic Journal*. 107(445) pp1815–1831.	**Research details:** Found on 21/6/2010 by uni infolinx > e journals > JSTOR > searched 'economics and happiness'. Also a copy in library (ref. only) JE201.2

Once you have completed your research log, sit back, take stock and give yourself a reward for all the hard work you have done so far. You have now completed the first stage of your research and have your own unique collection of sources that you know are exactly the right ones for the job.

Summary

- Having the confidence to select appropriate sources comes from a clear understanding of your assignment title and instructions and from knowing what you want from each source.

- Don't be afraid to reject texts for fear that you may be missing something or may need them later. There is not enough time to read everything and you will have to start discriminating sooner or later – better that it is sooner.

- It is *your* responsibility to check that your sources are relevant, appropriate and reliable for the type of information you need – this will usually mean using academically rigorous material.

- Use your university library.

- Keep a research log and nurture a sense of ownership of your own unique selection and collection of sources.

You are now in a good position to start reading in earnest and of course you should do this in a way that's interesting and enjoyable. However, you also want to read so that you maximise your understanding and your time, so think about what order to read your material in, perhaps something like:

first – sources that are central to your assignment, recent and simple

second – sources that are central, recent but more complex or difficult

third – texts that are older and less central

fourth – material that is older, less central and complex or difficult

Myth #4 You should read academic texts carefully from start to finish.

In reality there simply isn't enough time to read everything from cover to cover and you probably wouldn't want to anyway. We read different things in different ways. You quickly scan a train timetable for specific information but you follow a recipe carefully step by step (going back to check that you have done things correctly), and you read a novel from the beginning but in a much more relaxed way, skipping bits and even skipping to the end if you are finding it boring. For academic study you should apply the same principle that you use for anything else you read – matching the *way* you read something to *why* you are reading it.

Three different ways to read

1 **Scanning – looking over material quite quickly in order to pick out specific information**

   You might scan when you are browsing a database for texts on a specific topic or you might scan a text for specific information. You might also scan when you are looking back over material to check something.

2 **Gist reading – reading something fairly quickly in order to get the general idea or feel**

   You might do this by reading just the headings, introduction and conclusion or you might read for gist by going over the whole text fairly quickly. You might want to read for gist in order to decide whether to reject a text or read it in more detail. Reading for gist is also sometimes called skimming or reading for breadth.

3 Close reading – reading something in detail

You may want to read something in detail for several different reasons: as background reading; as a way in to a new and difficult topic; to make sure you understand discussions of data; or to clearly understand the detail or argument. Close reading is also called reading for depth.

Attention! It is important to remember that scanning or reading for gist is *not* a substitute for close reading. You *will* need to do a lot of detailed reading for academic work, and so the whole point of only scanning or gist reading some texts is to give you enough time for careful and close reading of the most important material. You therefore need to develop the skill of recognising when it is appropriate to scan, when to read for gist and when to do close, careful and reflective reading.

12 Stay flexible

Stay flexible about which reading method to use. You will often need to use combinations of methods, not just across different texts but also within a single text – zooming in and out. You might, for example, first quickly read over a whole text for gist, then read a section of it in detail, read some bits you find difficult again *very* carefully, and finally go back and scan the text for anything you think you may have missed.

Review your progress as you go along

You might also decide to change your reading approach as you read. After reading a quarter or a third of the text, ask yourself, 'Is it giving me what I want? Am I learning and thinking as I read? Do I understand what I'm reading?'

If the answer to these questions is 'no', then stop and think about why this is. It may be that you dived straight in with close reading and that it would be better to zoom out and get the general feel of the text first before going back to the detail. It may be that you need to find an easier text as a way in to the topic, or it may be that the material is not as relevant as you thought and that you should stop and move on to something else.

13 Plan the time to read

One of the main reasons why students get low marks in assignments is simply because they haven't spent enough time on all three parts of the process: reading, thinking and writing. You need to *care* about your reading, so give it a high priority.

- Get out of poor reading habits such as reading at times when you are rushed, tired or sleepy (reading for study just before bed is not a good idea either for reading or for sleeping!).
- Have both a short-term (e.g. weekly) time management plan for reading as well as a long-term one (over a semester or a whole year, including time for more relaxed background reading during holidays).
- Be clear to yourself and to others that you need *x* amount of time for reading and will be busy reading at *y* times. Make sure family and friends understand that reading for study is demanding, important work and not at all like reading for leisure.
- Find your own ideal concentration span that strikes a balance between reading for long enough to have a meaningful session and stopping before you lose concentration: for example, 30 minutes > 5 min break > another 30 mins > 5 min break > a final 30–40 mins.

- Mild time pressure can increase your motivation and therefore alertness, but don't put yourself under so much pressure that you rush and so don't really understand, question or reflect on what you read.

How quickly should you be reading?

There is no correct answer to this question. Understanding and thinking as you read is more important than speed, and how quickly you read a text will depend on why you are reading it. However, if you think you could do with reading a little faster, first work out roughly how quickly you read at the moment. Around 40 words per minute for an unfamiliar and difficult text and around 100+ words for an easy text is about average. You may find that your reading speed is fine as it is, but if you do want to increase your speed, try some of these techniques:

- Use a reading guide (e.g. a slim pointer) to keep your eyes moving forward on the page and try not to keep going back on what you have just read.

- Read in meaningful chunks, fixing your eyes only two or three times a line, rather than slowly reading every word.

- If you are in the habit of vocalising the words as you read, try doing this more quickly and in your head rather than out loud.

Before you start a reading session, deal with your current distractions and worries as best you can. Writing them down and deciding what actions you will take to deal with them will help unclutter your mind.

Make sure that you have everything you need to hand, that you have adequate light (but without glare) and that the text is roughly at eye level so that you are not bending your neck.

Some people work better listening to music (research has shown that if you do, it should be quiet and soft with a faster tempo). If you are in the habit of listening to music while you study, try working for a few days without it and see if in fact you read more effectively – you may not have had to concentrate on such difficult and demanding texts before.

On screen or on paper?

The jury is out as to whether it is better overall to read from screen or from paper, but here are some things to think about.

Paper	Screen
Pros:	**Pros:**
You can jot down notes, thoughts and questions and underline and highlight on the text, all without changing the original document.	May encourage you to read first and make notes from memory afterwards, making you more independent of the text.
You can easily see the whole text at once and flip between pages, giving you a good overall sense of the shape and structure of the text and how much there is to go!	You can alter the font type and font/background colour for easier reading. (If you find that letters and words 'jump around' on the page, try changing the font – Trebuchet MS, Arial, Comic Sans and Geneva for Macs are more readable fonts. You could also experiment with font and background colours. Try dark blue or violet fonts, and light yellow, light blue or light orange backgrounds.)
You can lay out and rearrange pages as you like to make your own connections.	
You can use your 'mouse hand' for writing and drinking tea while reading.	
You can read wherever/whenever you like.	

Paper	Screen
Cons:	*Cons:*
You have to borrow, buy or print out the material.	Reading on screen can feel more pressurised due to the fear that you may lose the webpage.
	Any annotations or font changes you make to the document will change it and so you won't have a copy of the original.
	It's slower to navigate through the text and skip back and forth and so less easy to see where you are, which can lead to a sense of feeling 'lost' in the text.
	It can be very tempting to cut and paste different bits of a document or bits of different documents together, and then use this edited version in your assignment. This is definitely not a good idea, as it defeats the whole purpose of academic study and can lead you down the path of plagiarism.
	Long stints at the screen are bad for your eyes.

Summary

- Your reading environment should balance comfort with alertness.

- Know what you want from each source before you read it.

- An effective reader is someone who can match their reading strategy to their reading purpose. If you are reading everything from start to finish at the same speed, you are doing something wrong.

- You need to find reading strategies that allow you to build up a 'detailed *and* broad knowledge base'.

- Be flexible and review your progress as you read to make sure that your purpose and methods remain appropriate.

- You will not enjoy or relish everything you read, but finding the answers to your questions and achieving your goals will bring its own satisfaction.

PART 4

READING, QUESTIONING AND EVALUATING

Part 4 starts with two extracts: Extract 1 is from a source for Assignment 1 (p15) and Extract 2 is from a source for Assignment 2 (p16).

With each extract I have given examples of an *active reading approach*: the pre- and post-reading *thinking* you should do, and the use of clues in the text *structure, language* and *table/chart information* when reading. Below is a summary list of the annotations.

Extract 1: clues in the structure	**Extract 2: clues in the data**
① title	• What is measured
② subtitle	• What is shown – key statistics
③ numbering and lists	• Who collected the data, when and where
④ use of paragraphs (especially first and last)	• What is shown – key statistics
	• What is measured

Extract 2: clues in the language	**Extract 2: clues in the language**
⑤ verbs that show what the author thinks	⑩ checking what the verbs in the sentence refer to
⑥ linking/contrasting words	⑪ phrases that indicate minor points
⑦ words you need to know to understand the text	⑫ checking what words such as *this/that* refer to
⑧ phrases that indicate rephrasing of a point	⑬ words important for understanding the argument
⑨ words you can look up after reading	

Extract 1

Misconceptions and misinformation: The problems with Guideline Daily Amounts (GDAs)

A review of GDAs and their use for signalling nutritional information on food and drink labels.

Report written by: Dr Tim Lobstein, Jane Landon and Paul Lincoln
with contributions from: Dr Ruth Ash and Dr Vivienne Press
National Heart Forum, February 2007

....

① Title gives the authors' position (problems with GDAs)

② Subtitle summarises what the report does

Introduction

This report assesses the use of Guideline Daily Amounts (GDAs) on food and drink packages as a means of conveying nutritional information. It finds several areas of concern. This use of percentage GDA signals on front-of-pack labelling has been promoted by some sections of the food industry as an alternative to a 'traffic-light' signposting system recommended by the Food Standards Agency (FSA). This report concludes that GDA signals are not the optimum method for helping consumers make quick, informed choices for at least six good reasons:

1. The GDA values do not distinguish maximum, minimum and average recommended amounts.
2. GDA values for adults and for children are used inconsistently, and adult GDAs are sometimes used on child-targeted products.
3. The GDAs used for labelling are based on values which are not the most suitable either for public health policy or for individuals.
4. The GDA displays are based on arbitrary portion sizes.
5. GDA signals for different nutrients are sometimes included or left out in an arbitrary and confusing manner.
6. The standard GDA signals lack colour coding for quick consumer appraisal and interpretation.

③ Numbered reasons that support the argument

These problems in the construction and use of GDA front-of-pack signals undermine the ability to provide clear and consistent signals to consumers as a means of promoting better public health. The FSA traffic-light signposting system is better able to provide a clear signal to consumers at the point of purchase.

④ Last paragraph of intro. summarises the argument

<u>Post-reading thinking - evaluation after reading the report:</u>
Report gives informed, logical and persuasive argument, but National Heart Forum may be biased towards the traffic light system. Worth reading - aims to influence government policy?

Extract 2

Happiness and Economic Performance
Author: Andrew J. Oswald

Source: The Economic Journal, Vol. 107, No. 445 (Nov., 1997) pp. 1815-1831 Published by: Blackwell Publishing for the Royal Economic Society Stable pp 1820–1822

....

The British Household Panel Survey data show that income has no strong role to play, [in individual well-being] but that joblessness does. Clark and Oswald (1994) fail to find any statistically significant effect from income. The sharp impact of unemployment, however, is illustrated by …. data on 6,000 British workers in 1991. Mental distress is twice as high among the unemployed as among those who have work. Interestingly, research suggests that the worst thing about losing one's job is not the drop in take-home income. It is the non-pecuniary distress. To put this differently, most regression results imply that an enormous amount of extra income would be required to compensate people for having no work.

Table 5   *The Microeconomics of Happiness in Europe: 1975–86*

	All	**Unemployed**
Very happy (%)	23.4	15.9
Pretty happy (%)	57.9	51.1
Not too happy (%)	18.6	33.0
	Lowest income quartile people	**Highest-income quartile people**
Very happy (%)	18.8	28.4
Pretty happy (%)	54.5	58.5
Not too happy (%)	26.7	13.1

Source: Di Tella et al. (1996) using Eurobarometer data.
Total sample 108,802 observations.

All people in the sample of 108,802 compared with only the unemployed people in the same sample.

Less than a fifth of the <u>whole sample</u> were 'not too happy' but less than a third of the <u>unemployed people</u> in the sample were 'not too happy'.

Double the number of people on low income were 'not too happy' compared to the people on a high income.

You will find the full details of primary sources in the list of references. Note that the research was conducted over 14 years ago.

<u>Post-reading thinking</u>: Do the statistics about people on low and high income support Oswald's argument? How does this data compare with today?

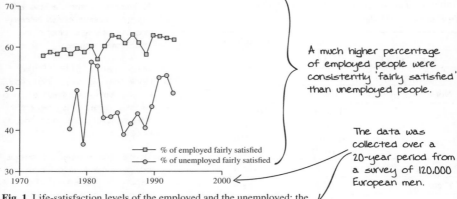

A much higher percentage of employed people were consistently 'fairly satisfied' than unemployed people.

The data was collected over a 20-year period from a survey of 120,000 European men.

Fig. 1 Life-satisfaction levels of the employed and the unemployed: the European countries 1970s–1990s. *Notes.* The vertical axis measures the proportion of people saying they were 'fairly satisfied with life' as a whole. The data source is the Eurobarometer Surveys, which provide a random sample here of approximately 120,000 European men. Running a trend line through each series produces almost exactly the same gradient, namely, just over 0.2.

<u>Post-reading thinking</u>: There was a very sharp fall in happiness in unemployed men in the late 1970s followed by a very sharp rise in the early 1980s - how might this be explained? Would women have followed a similar pattern?

Eurobarometer data, in Table 5 and Fig. 1, also show that the unemployed feel much less satisfied with life,[6] and indicate that the relative distress from unemployment does not appear to be trending downwards through the years (the 'unhappiness gap' is not secularly shrinking). In passing this might be thought to raise doubts about the oft-expressed view that an increasingly generous welfare state is somehow at the root of Europe's economic problems.

A review of psychologists' earlier work is available in Warr et al. (1988). The upshot of all this evidence is:

FINDING 3. Unemployed people are very unhappy.

(Conclusion page 1828)

The conclusions of the paper do not mean that economic forces have little impact on people's lives. A consistent theme through the paper's different forms of evidence has been the vulnerability of human beings to joblessness. Unemployment appears to be the ordinary economic source of unhappiness. If so, economic growth should not be a government's primary concern.

Handwritten margin notes:

⑩ These verbs link to 'data'

⑪ Indicates a side point

⑫ Refers to the fact that the 'unhappiness gap' is not shrinking

⑬ Important word for understanding the context of the argument accurately

<u>Post-reading thinking - evaluation after reading the article:</u> Expert author, persuasive argument - worth reading. But some of the evidence is perhaps selective and Oswald makes generalisations? I need to find further evidence from other sources.

Chapters 15 to 19 look in more detail at what you need to think about when you are reading.

Have a clear purpose

You should by now have an idea of the author's general purpose in writing the text (An introduction to a topic? An academic discussion of ideas? Presenting new research?) and you should already know why *you* want to read it. Having a clear goal in mind as you read will really sharpen your focus and so increase your motivation.

Make predictions

Make some predictions about what you think the text will say. If the topic is new to you, use the title and sub-headings to help you come up with some predictions. It doesn't matter if your predictions are sometimes wrong – it's the predicting itself that will get your active reading muscles working.

Build a scaffold, engage and enjoy

If you are not initially interested in the topic, try to *become* interested. What do you already know about the subject? What are the questions and issues that surround it and how does it relate to your life experiences?

Use the clues in the text structure

Get out of the habit (if you are in it) of just glancing over headings and sub-headings – try instead to read them and reflect on what they say about the author's message. Read the introduction and conclusion and the first line of each paragraph (this usually gives you the key idea of that paragraph) to get a general idea of the author's message before you drill down to the detail. Keep an eye out for words and phrases in bold or italics – these usually indicate a key point.

Be clear on what different parts of the text are doing

It is crucial that you can distinguish between description, explanation and argument – otherwise you won't be able to get a clear picture of what is going on in the text.

▶ **Description**: Describes but does *not* give reasons why something is, and does *not* try to judge or persuade the reader of something.

> *For example*: 'This report assesses the use of Guideline Daily Amounts (GDAs) on food and drink packages as a means of conveying nutritional information.'

- **Explanation**: *Does* give reasons for something (and may also give a conclusion) but does *not* try to judge or persuade the reader of something.

    For example: 'This use of percentage GDA signals on front-of-pack labeling has been promoted by some sections of the food industry as an alternative to a "traffic-light" signposting system recommended by the Food Standards Agency (FSA).'

- **Argument**: An argument proposes a statement *and* gives reasons and evidence that lead to a particular conclusion *and* uses these reasons and conclusion to persuade the reader of a particular idea or action.

    For example: 'This report concludes that GDA signals are not the optimum method for helping consumers make quick, informed choices for at least six good reasons ... These problems in the construction and use of GDA front-of-pack signals undermine the ability to provide clear and consistent signals to consumers as a means of promoting better public health. The FSA traffic-light signposting system is better able to provide a clear signal to consumers at the point of purchase.'

Difference between opinion and argument

Opinion, agreement and disagreement are points of view (perhaps trying to persuade) *without* supporting evidence or logical reasoning. Opinion and dis/agreement are *not* valid arguments.

An example of an opinion would be: 'We don't think that the GDA labeling system is an effective method of reducing diet-related diseases.'

Don't get distracted from the main message

If the text has an argument, try to identify this and separate it out from other types of information such as background information or examples. However, you do need to understand the argument accurately and in context, so also read the sentences before and after the key points.

Don't get distracted by side-points, examples or 'special facts' boxes put in to make the text look more interesting, and don't mistake these for the actual argument.

Use the language clues

▶ Look out for language 'signposts' which tell you that a main point is coming up.

> *For example*: There are three main problems … First, … second … finally …
>
> The question/issue/point is …
>
> The main cause/effect/result/effect/implication/flaw is …
>
> Importantly, …
>
> My argument is that …

▶ The author may use language signposts to indicate that s/he is repeating or rephrasing an important point.

> *For example*: In other words/so/to put this differently/another way of saying this is …

▶ Look at the *verbs* the author uses, as these give big clues to what they are doing:

> *For example*: I suggest/propose [setting out their argument]
>
> I have proven/shown/established/demonstrated [summarising their points]
>
> I question/query/challenge/dispute/reject [disagreeing with someone else]
>
> They claim that/fail to [*about* to disagree with someone else]

▶ Be aware of how authors use the words 'may/might/possibly/tends to' to indicate how definite they are about their claim or how strong they think a correlation is:

For example: This suggests that > This *might* suggest that > This *may possibly* suggest that >

Use the data clues

Take a few moments to study the data and note the essential points – a great short cut to understanding the text. Look at how this works on pages 61 and 62.

Make sure you have understood *accurately*

> ✅ 'Sources used accurately and concisely …'
> ❌ 'inaccurate reading and limited understanding …'

Precision is crucial in academic work so be careful not to misinterpret the text. Common student pitfalls include:

▶ Misinterpreting comparatives or superlatives such as *the best/greatest/worst/one of.*
   For example, it would be wrong to say that Lobstein et al. think the traffic-light system is the *only* effective food labelling system – they are only saying that it is *better* than the GDA system. It would also be wrong to say that they view arbitrary portion size as the problem with GDAs – they state that it is *one of* the problems.

- Being inaccurate about the degree of something.

  For example, it would be incorrect to say that Oswald states that economic forces have a huge impact on happiness. Oswald does not in fact say how much economic forces affect happiness, just that they do have an effect.

- Overlooking the words *not* or *no*.

  For example, the word *not* in the following sentence is crucial. 'This report concludes that the GDA signals are not the optimum method for helping consumers make quick informal choices …' Be careful not to mistakenly reverse the author's meaning.

- Being imprecise in who says what.

  For example, it would be incorrect to say that Oswald's findings show that income does not significantly affect happiness – this finding came from research conducted by Clark and Oswald.

- Not being precise enough in describing data from graphs, diagrams and tables.

If you are not sure whether you have understood a text properly, check with a tutor or other students on your course.

Make up your own mind

☑ '... willingness to engage critically with the literature and ability to go beyond it ...'

☒ '... does not go beyond the assertion of points derived from the literature'

☑ '... ability to analyse materials and their implications'

But don't you think that...?
Really? But what do you mean by...?
What makes you say that?
And your point is?

Critical thinking

Myth #5 There is only one correct way to understand a text.

Myth #6 You can't really disagree with an academic text because you are not an expert in that subject.

Although you need to understand what the author is saying on the page, you also need to go beyond this level of understanding and decide what *you* think about the author's message. You need to ask questions of the text and then form your own reasoned views on its argument, importance and implications. This is called *critical thinking* or *critical analysis*.

1 Be aware of your own context

We all bring our own context to anything we read – our individual bias, perspective and experience – and we need to be aware of these in order to judge a text fairly. For example, do you have an underlying belief that wealth *does* make people happy and if so, how does this influence your views on Oswald's argument?

2 Be aware of the author's context

Authors are also human beings and so will also have their own context. Find out who the author is and who they work for (Google is useful for this). Find out what historical, political and social context they are/were writing in and whether they have a particular ideological stance (e.g. Marxist, conservative, feminist). How might these contexts affect what the author hoped to achieve?

For example, the report on GDA food labelling was written on behalf of the National Heart Forum. The NHF is composed of various charities, scientists and practitioners in the field who help inform government policy and the FSA. The authors of the report may therefore be biased towards the traffic-light labelling system as opposed to the food manufacturer's GDA system.

3 Challenge the author and identify assumptions, gaps and flaws

As you read (perhaps at a second reading) engage the author in a conversation in your mind and challenge them. Remember that thinking critically does not mean that you *have* to disagree with what they say – you might disagree or you might agree. You also do need to try to understand the author's point of view before you can challenge it.

▶ What assumptions is the author's argument based on and do you think these are correct? For example, one main underlying assumption in the Oswald text extract (as apparent from the conclusion) is that it is the government's role to decrease unemployment.

- Look at the author's use of evidence. Do their reasons and conclusion link together logically or are there gaps or flaws in the argument?

  For example, does the data in Table 5 on page 61 really support Oswald's argument? Also, Oswald claims that 'Unemployed people are very unhappy' yet the data on which Oswald bases this claim is collected from men only (read the small print under Fig.1 on page 62).

- How primary data and other research have been used in secondary sources is particularly important in science. Check who the research team of a paper work for. Is their bibliography correct and are they aware of other current research in the field? Have proper controls and error analyses been conducted? Could there be other explanations for their correlations and conclusions? Could they have done things in a more efficient way?

- Be aware of opinion, agreement or disagreement that is not supported by evidence and reasoning. Phrases such as *surely/we have to remember/it is perfectly clear that/it is obvious that/it is a fact that/one can't fail to recognise that* are sometimes used to persuade the reader that something is true without providing any actual evidence. Emotive phrases such as *completely/absolutely/merely/hardly/only* are also sometimes used as 'empty persuaders'.

4 Evaluate

After your critical analysis, stand back, reflect and give the text a final evaluation. What is the way of thinking of the author? What is the text trying to do and how well does it do it? Why do you think people read this text? Do *you* think it is worth reading and why?

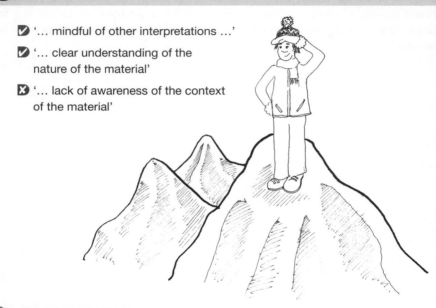

✓ '... mindful of other interpretations ...'

✓ '... clear understanding of the nature of the material'

✗ '... lack of awareness of the context of the material'

Location, location, location!

After reflecting on the specific text you have read, relate it to the other material you have read on that topic. As you read more, you need to build up a mental picture of the 'location' of different authors. How do the texts differ and how are they similar? Where does each author 'sit' in the subject? Which authors agree with each other and which disagree? Are there any authors who are 'out there' with their own novel idea? Who are the Old Masters and who are the emerging stars?

Develop your understanding

Don't underestimate the importance of discussing your reading and ideas with other students and with your tutors. Make the most of seminars and study groups, and use reference lists and bibliographies from key texts to find relevant further reading. Discussing different angles and interpretations is a key part of understanding the context and nature of your material – the wider picture.

Myth #7 If you don't understand something or feel confused, it is probably because you are being a bit thick.

Feeling confused?

Reading means learning new things, and feeling a bit nervous and confused can in fact be a sign that your brain is absorbing, learning and fitting in the new information with the old – a good and normal process! New learning and understanding takes time. Even professors find some texts difficult and have to re-read them, look up words they don't know and use other techniques to help them get to grips with new material.

- Brainstorm on the topic and relate it to what you already know before you start reading in order to activate the relevant scaffold in your brain.
- If you are getting stuck or find yourself reading the same sentence over and over again, have a break and then write a short summary or reflection on what you have read so far. This will help your brain assimilate the new information and when you

go back to your reading, you will usually discover that you now understand more clearly.

Difficult text?

Myth #8 Intelligent people and good readers usually only need to read things once.

If you feel (or have been told) that you are not a great reader, this is probably due to lack of experience, practice and good reading strategies rather than a lack of intelligence. If you find yourself struggling with a difficult text, it could also be because the chapter or article you are reading is poorly written!

- Remember the process of purpose > motivation > understanding. Not having a clear purpose can make you feel anxious and restless and easily distracted by familiar things such as housework or watching TV.

- If you are losing motivation, remind yourself of your initial reasons for choosing the text, module and even course.

- If the text is complex and dense, find an easier way in, such as zooming out before going back to the detail, reading simpler texts on the topic or discussing the text with a colleague or tutor.

- If you really have tried but just can't understand a particular text, try not to feel stressed about it and just move on to a different one.

Dealing with words you don't understand

> **Myth #9** You should look up all the words you don't understand as you go along.

Don't look up every unknown word as you read as this will slow you down and break your concentration. Look up the words you think you need to understand the text and just underline the others to look up later (but do look them up).

There is no magic pill for developing your word knowledge, and exhaustive research has shown that we learn new words over time by – you guessed it – reading. However, for academic study you will need to speed up your vocabulary development, and there are several things you can do to achieve this:

- Don't just learn the word on the page. To be able to actively use a word you need to know its other forms (e.g. noun, adjective, verb, negative) and which words are always or usually used before and after it (e.g. in/at/on). It's also useful to learn other words that have the same meaning (synonyms).

- Buy and *use* a good dictionary and read through the guide at the front. A good dictionary will give you most of the information you need to be able to use a word properly.

- Make a note of useful words and phrases that keep coming up and practise using them precisely. A common student error is to use words in a nearly but not quite right way.

Dealing with sentences you don't understand

Academic texts should be written in a clear style although you will occasionally come across overly long and complex sentences that have several different parts such as this one.

Tips for unpacking difficult sentences:

1 Break it down into its separate parts. Sentences are usually divided by commas or semi-colons or words such as *and/or/but/although/which/that/such as*. Our example sentence can be broken down into four parts:

Academic texts should be written in a clear style

although you will occasionally come across overly long and complex sentences

that have several different parts

such as this one.

2 Find the subjects and verbs in the sentence that go together.

3 Check that you are clear on the meaning of words that *link* sentences or parts of a sentence

E.g. *however/nevertheless/despite/although/whereas/moreover/ also/in addition.*

4 Be clear about what words such as *it/these/they/this/this one/which/that/such* are referring to.

5 Read the sentences before and after the problematic one.

6 Write out the sentence in your own words.

 READING AND MAKING NOTES

Summary

- Make sure you are clear on the function and structure of the whole text and of its different parts so that you can clearly separate out the key information or argument.

- If you are finding a text difficult, recognise your feelings, accept that they are normal and then use specific strategies to move forward.

- You will not develop your vocabulary through some kind of magic – you need to be proactive.

- Have the confidence to know that your course reading *will* get easier with time and practice.

- Develop a critical approach in order to come to your own reasoned views about the author's message.

- Identifying the similarities and differences between texts and author objectives is the final step in really grasping the nature of your material.

MAKING NOTES

Why make notes?

The physical and mental process of making notes enables your brain to absorb, reflect and make connections between different bits of knowledge in your mind, leading to a much better understanding of your reading.

Making your own notes (rather than just highlighting or cutting and pasting) will also:

- help you concentrate
- keep you motivated by tracking and signalling progress
- help you remember information more easily
- start you on the process of using your own words and style
- give you your own unique record of the text
- save you time when it comes to writing your assignment
- result in a better assignment that gets higher marks.

If you don't make notes and just go straight from the text to writing your assignment, you will be bypassing key elements in the critical thinking process, and you will find it harder to develop your own independent understanding.

Have a clear purpose

To be effective, your notes need to be *purposeful* and *meaningful*. A clear purpose is just as important for note making as it is for reading – your notes should address the questions you want answered. Think also about the function you want your notes to fulfil. Do you want your notes to:

- extract all the essential points and arguments?
- note down only information on a specific theme?
- focus only on information that addresses your own angle or question?
- clarify the way the points relate to each other and see how the ideas are organised?
- reorganise or connect the information in a new way?

You write notes for yourself, not an outside audience; however, whatever your notes look like, they should always have the following key features.

Key feature	Why?
Full reference details (similar to a research log entry) and the relevant page numbers	You will only be able to use your notes in your assignment if you can give full reference details. Reference details will also help you find sources if you need to check back. Make sure you note down when the author of the text cites *other* authors.
Information on when/where you made the notes	This will help you recall associations and trains of thought later.
Your purpose and questions written at the top of your notes	This will keep your notes focused and help stop you from taking notes that you don't need and will never use. If you are worried about needing information at a later date, just write down a key word/phrase and then you can use your research log to find the details later if you need to.

Key feature	Why?
Information that is not too detailed or too brief	If your notes are too brief, the meaning will be unclear and you won't understand them in a month's or year's time. If your notes are too detailed then it probably means you are copying from the text – note making does not mean copying whole sections from the text.
Clear distinction between the main points/argument and minor points/examples	If you find you can't separate out the main points, it means that you don't really understand the text. Think about whether you even need to make notes on minor points.
Meaningful use of abbreviations	Using abbreviations will help prevent copying and will encourage you to use your own style. Keep a record of what key abbreviations mean.
A clear system for distinguishing between: **exact phrases from the text (quotations)**	You must keep careful track of quotations (even very short ones) in your notes to make sure that you reference them in your final assignment – use colour, quotations marks or write them in a separate space.

Key feature	Why?
mostly the same words from the text, or a mixture of your words and those from the text (close paraphrase)	Again, keep a careful track of this – for your assignment you will need to rewrite these bits so that they are completely or almost completely (90%) in your own words.
your *own* words to describe information from the text (paraphrase)	Do try to use your own words and style as much as possible. You may be worried about changing the meaning of the text, of 'moving away' from it, or feel that you can't put things into your own words as well as the original. However, using at least some your own words in your notes will help you to start the paraphrasing process. Your confidence will increase with practice.
your own comments and ideas	It's a good idea to have a separate column or space for these.
White space	In case you need to add anything later.

22 Top tips for making notes

Read first, note later

Try reading the text first *without* making any notes and then summarise it in your mind or out loud. Make notes without looking back at the text and then go back to it if you need to check anything.

Go easy on the highlighter

If you really do want to mark the text at a first reading, just pick out the most relevant sections by putting a line down alongside them, using a pencil rather than a highlighter. You probably won't really get a clear idea of the key points of a text until you have got to the end; therefore if you highlight as you read for the first time, you may be stuck with highlighting that you later want to change. A better use of the highlighter might be to use it on your notes for bringing out key points.

Do more than just annotate

Annotating a text is fine, but also try to write notes that are separate from the text. Online note-making software usually only allows you to make short annotations on or around the text and so, again, also make your own notes either on a separate e-document or on paper.

Explain your reactions to yourself

It's good to react to the text, but don't just put **!!** or **?** in the margin – write out clearly and precisely what your thoughts are.

Avoid secretary syndrome

Myth #10 Good notes should have all the points from the text copied down.

You should *make* notes, not *take* notes. Unless you are trying to learn something by heart, there isn't much point in copying down lots of individual sentences or chunks from the text; this usually means that you are on auto pilot rather than actively reading and thinking. Try to build up the confidence to read and think first and then make notes in your own words that address your own questions. Only copy down phrases as quotations if they are really special and powerful.

Write short summary comments

As you make notes, write short summaries in your own words. Your choice of verbs in these summaries should accurately reflect what the author is doing in the text. For example: 'Lobstein et al. *describe* the problems with GDAs …' or 'Oswald *interprets* the data …'

Experiment with different note formats

▶ **Mind maps** are excellent for brainstorming what you already know (or even for sketching out an essay plan) before you start reading. You can then identify the gaps in your knowledge and the questions you want answered by sources.

▶ **Pattern/visual notes** can really help you to remember information and are good for understanding argument structure and for making connections. Make sure that pattern/visual notes still include the key features listed in Chapter 21, including page numbers and distinctions between your own words and quotations.

▶ **Linear/bullet point notes** are an easy format when using a computer and are good for clarifying hierarchy of information.

▶ **Using note cards** for different points allows you to reorganise the information in different ways to make new and original connections. Note cards can be useful if you are in the habit of making too many notes, as you can go through each card and reject ones that are not relevant.

▶ **Using more than one format.** For example, if you usually take linear/list notes, try making pattern notes *from* your linear notes to really familiarise yourself with the information and to make new connections.

Some examples of good and poor notes

Examples of good notes

Here's an example of some good linear notes from the report extract on GDAs. Notice that the student has not copied down any quotations but has used their own words. They have also used a separate column for their own comments and thoughts.

Misconceptions and misinformation: The problems with Guideline Daily Amounts (GDAs)
Lobstein T, Landon J and Lincoln P. National Heart Forum, February 2007.
Found via NHF website www.heartforum.org.uk on 19/6/2010
Notes made on 21/6/2010

My comments/questions	Notes on text
My Qs – Food labelling as CHD prev. measure.	
Probs. with GDAs and preventing CHD? Solutions? Other measures?	
p.1 Intro – gives a summary but I will need to look at the evidence in the full report.	
Q – why were food manfs. allowed to dev. and use their own system – finance and political lobbying??	% GDAs on front labels – dev/promoted by food manfs. as alt. to FSA system (traffic light).
Does the report give solid evidence for these claims? Lobstein may be biased.	There are real probs. with GDA – at least 6 –
	e.g. give no recs. for min. avg. or max. portions
	sometimes adult GDAs used on food that children usually eat.

These probs. are pretty bad if true!	Nutritional info. smts arbitrary (because manfs. want to keep product distinctions).
My summary of the main argument –	**My summary:**
	GDAs are sometimes arbitrary and confusing for consumers and so not effective in helping them make healthy eating choices. The FSA traffic light system is clearer to consumers and so more effective in promoting healthy eating.
Follow-on Q – why/how is FSA system better/clearer?	

Here's a second example of some effective notes, this time pattern notes on the extract from the Oswald article. Notice that the student has only copied down one sentence and has put it in quotation marks.

Oswald AJ (1997) Happiness and Economic Performance.
The Economic Journal 107 (445), p1815–31.   Found from Infolinx → ejournals → JSTOR.
Notes – pp 1815 & 1828. Made on 20/6/2

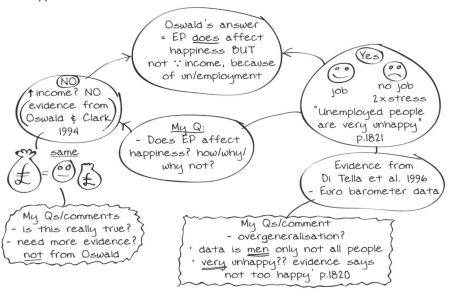

An example of some poor notes

Here are some linear notes on the Oswald extract that are not so good. They don't have adequate reference details and are a mixture of copied sentences and meaningless phrases. They don't distinguish between the student's and the author's words or between major and minor points. They lack space for the student's own comments and – worst of all – do not express the main point of the text.

Oswald AJ. **Happiness and Economic Performance.**
- British Household Panel survey data show that income has no strong role to play.
- mental stress is twice as high among the unemployed as among those who have work.
- the gap is not shrinking.
- raises doubts about the view that an increasingly generous welfare state is at the root of Europe's economic problems.

Unemployed people are very unhappy.

Always review your notes. It has been shown that students who look back over their notes to check for clarity and meaning, and who reflect on them, are more successful learners. Look again at your assignment title and check the focus and relevance of your notes. Familiarise yourself with them and start to put them to work. Ways of doing this include:

- reworking your notes using a different format – linear to pattern or vice versa
- reorganising your notes around your assignment question title, adding comments and identifying any knowledge gaps
- reorganising your notes around your own unique question or angle to help develop your own 'voice'
- using your notes to write an annotated bibliography
- **using your notes to write a short critical reflection**: This can be extremely useful. The reflection can be informal but it's a good idea to write it in your own words, in full sentences and to use quotation marks for exact phrases from the text. Include a short summary of what you have learnt (if the text has a diagram or data try to summarise this in one sentence) and also include your thoughts from your questioning, evaluation and location of the text.

A reflection will help you to restate the author's information and ideas in your own words and will enable you to further develop your *own* ideas. It will help you to relate what you have read to what you already know, and will put you in a position where you can see why, how and where you want to use your sources in your assignment.

An example of a short reflection

> Oswald argues that economic performance *does* affect people's happiness, but only because it influences employment rates. He argues that it is whether people have a job or not that has a significant effect on their well-being, not income. I think this is a very interesting finding and not one I had expected. I can see how this would be the case but I think that Oswald is exaggerating his claim. His evidence has some flaws in it and his finding that 'Unemployed people are very unhappy' seems to me to be over-simplified. The data he uses in fact only looks at men and also does not say that people without jobs are *very* unhappy – also I know some unemployed people who are very happy!
>
> Still, Oswald is clearly an authority in this field, has published widely and the background notes give details of where I can find more evidence for his claim. I will probably use this article as a main source in my essay but I will check out more closely some of the data Oswald uses and will also try to find authors that argue against him.

Things to be careful of when using your notes

Accidental collusion

- **Collaboration** is when you are *explicitly* required to work with others. Keep a record of what you have shared with the group and make sure that your final assignment clearly states what collaboration took place.
- **Collusion** is when you work with others in a hidden way and is a form of cheating. Be careful not to accidentally take part in collusion – don't lend your notes or other written work to other students if you are supposed to be working individually.

Accidental plagiarism

Be sure to always show clearly when you have used words *and/or ideas and information* from your reading. Even when you express information completely in your own words (paraphrasing), you *must* give a reference both in the body of your assignment and also in the bibliography.

Be careful not to imply that you have read something when you have not! If the article you read by author X mentions author Y, you must put something such as 'Y cited in X' in your assignment to show that you have only actually read the article by author X.

Misrepresenting the author

If you use an author's argument in your essay, don't use their material out of context. Be aware of how the bit you are using fits into the author's whole argument and present this context clearly. For example, you would be misrepresenting Oswald if you said that he views economic growth as not important.

Don't let your sources take control

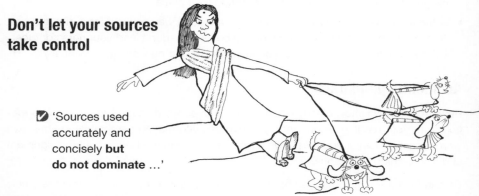

☑ 'Sources used
accurately and
concisely **but
do not dominate ...**'

Avoid writing an assignment that consists mainly of large chunks of written-up notes sewn together by only thin threads of your own sentences. Try to make *your* argument and voice stand out as the dominant one, and make your notes work for you as evidence in support of *your* answer to the assignment title. Your aim is to meet the expectations and marking criteria at the top of the well-built assignment wall:

'Evaluates evidence and synthesises materials clearly to develop persuasive arguments.'

'Evidence used appropriately to support their conclusion.'

Summary

- Students who have a clear purpose for making notes, who separate out more important from less important information, and who use their own words, are more successful learners.

- Notes should *not* be chunks of slightly changed copying, but the start of the process of expressing your own 'way of understanding'.

- Experiment with different note formats and try using more than one format for different stages of your reading and note making.

- Writing a short reflection from your notes will consolidate your reading and thinking and will maximise the effectiveness of the whole reading and note-making process.

- Notes that directly address your assignment title and your own questions in your own words, and that include your own comments, can almost act as the first draft of your assignment.

- Develop a sense of ownership of your notes. It should be *your* voice your tutor hears when reading your assignment, and developing your own voice should start at the note-making stage.

Final comment

I hope that you have found this pocket guide useful. Anything worthwhile you read should have an impact on other aspects of your life and on your world view. Believe it or not, writing for academic work does involve creativity, and if you have an active and engaged approach to reading and note making, you will be surprised at the new and creative thoughts and questions you can generate.

Appendix 1: Examples of common abbreviations for note making

Full word or phrase	Abbreviation or symbol	Full word or phrase	Abbreviation or symbol
and/plus	+	maximum	max.
approximately	approx.	minimum	min.
because	∵	minus	−
compare	cf.	number	no. or #
decrease	↘	pages	pp.
different from/unlike	≠	regarding	re.
for example	e.g.	results from	←
government	gov.	results in/leads to	→
greater than/more than	>	same as/ditto	"
important	imp.	similar to	≈
in other words, namely	i.e.	therefore	∴
increase	↗	versus	vs.
information	info.	very	v.
less than/smaller than	<	with reference to	re.
like/equal to	=		

 Appendix

Appendix 2: Definitions of words used in this guide

acknowledge To indicate that a source has been used and to give information on that source. A common way of acknowledging an author is to give a reference (see below).

annotated bibliography A brief summary and evaluation of a text that comments on the author's background, the context and intended audience of the text, and its value and contribution to the subject.

annotation A comment, explanation or additional piece of information added to a text.

article A separate piece of writing in a larger publication. Common types of articles are newspaper articles, magazine articles and academic articles in academic journals.

cite, to To mention (and usually give information on) an author. A common way of citing is to give a reference. The word *citation* is also sometimes used to mean a quotation.

primary source The first, original source of information or ideas.

reference Information about a source. You give a reference in your assignment (an in-text reference) and also in your reference list.

secondary source A source which writes about, discusses or uses a previously written primary source.

Index